eros rex

PRAISE FOR *EROS REX*

"Haley Hodges' *Eros Rex* is a bold and electric debut, sparkling with music, metaphysical seeking, and carnal yearning. These desirous, winsome, provocative poems relish in the pleasures of rhyme and delight with their surprising proximities of archaic and contemporary speech, exploring Christian devotion through a refreshingly sexy lens. Flirtatious and profound, Hodges has written this book for all of us who 'require a book of uncommon prayer / with a spine of real bone.'"
Gabrielle Bates, author of *Judas Goat*

"With wit, wisdom, and remarkable jazz, Haley Hodges' debut collection, *Eros Rex*, proves to be a genuine interrogation of appearances, keen to apprehend the heart of the matter, the heart of our matter, accompanied by resilient joy, a deep and not-to-be-denied joy."
Scott Cairns, author of *Slow Pilgrim* and *Chemo with Coleridge*

"In this stunning debut collection, Haley Hodges probes the carnal aspects of Incarnation with unflinching honesty, disarming wit, and consummate craftsmanship. In poems that are both fierce and tender—often at the same time—Hodges considers how the hungers of the body and the hungers of the soul are so often present and noshing at the same table. Augustine knew this; so did Flannery O'Connor, and, more recently, poets like Anne Sexton, Marie Howe, and Kim Addonizio, and the poems in *Eros Rex* fit comfortably in this lineage. What makes them unique is the stark mirror of self-examination Hodges holds up to her subject: the remembrance—part sacred, part profane—of a profound consummation, in poems marked by anguish, resilience, and arresting beauty."
Jennifer Maier, author of *Now, Now* and *The Occupant*

eros rex

poems

haley hodges

Eros Rex
Copyright © 2026 by Haley Hodges
All rights reserved.

ISBN: 978-1-949039-70-2

Orison Books
PO Box 8385
Asheville, NC 28814
www.orisonbooks.com

Cover art: charcoal drawings by Sarah Dehn.
Used by permission of the artist.

Cover design by Luke Hankins and Addison Skigen.

Manufactured in the U.S.A.

CONTENTS

Eros Rex / 1
Burger King / 2
Sapiosexual / 3
Year Of / 4
Book of Uncommon Prayer / 6
Master, Master / 7
Blizzard / 8
Good Animal / 9
Heart Talks / 10
Two Takes / 11
Known / 12
Innocence / 13
Drifting / 14
What Was the Best You Ever Had? / 15
What Is Memory, if Not Testament? / 16
My Favorite Men / 17
Between the Jaws / 19
Salome / 20
Swamp Creed / 21
Moses / 22
Leaf Blower / 23
To the Other Haley in the Cab / 24
Back Yard / 26
Rooftop / 27
Lamb Legs / 28
Subservient / 29
Lesson / 30
Into Gold / 31
Maybe Welcome It, / 32
Inked / 33

Utterances / 34
Daddy Delilah / 35
Last Rites / 36
The Telling / 37
Alms / 38

Acknowledgments / 40
About the Author / 41
About Orison Books / 42

To my friends, for the lifeboat of your love.

Especially Bethany, Charlotte, Dan, Caroline, Jahdiel, and Frog who urged me—from the very beginning—to poetry.

EROS REX

Lord, we all carry
your world, wait
with its weight, which makes
a world in us, bores

holes in us, creates
a hole-world—better,
I guess, than void, than
none—but

I want to have my fill, to have
my fun. I want my fullness.

Instead I'm carrying
your chasm.
Come climax
Christ, come Eros Rex,
psyche's ecstasy, spasm
of the panting soul and opener
of the shut.

Enter my dark welkin,
fill, fulfill. Glut.

BURGER KING

Who are you
among the considerable oblivion
of plastic mustard packets, among the five-
dollar duo deals? Do seraphs even now
alight over my Whopper? A thought
as I cross the greying asphalt grime
of the parking lot—*surely the LORD*
is in this place, and I knew it not.

SAPIOSEXUAL

Clever girl, well done. Only feed me
that phrase from the hands of my
choosing—what wouldn't I give, be,
what wouldn't I suffer for rich food,
for this Turkish delight in throbbing
synapses, this simple utterance said
thickly, a red velvet ribbon for my lush
brain hair. And see how it makes me
glisten elsewhere, yes look how
good how pliant my mouth my hands
my shuddering mind! I speak to you—
you who fill neurotransmissions
with dates and citrus, with heavy
spices and figs, you that seek to cast
squealing cerebral pigs before one swollen
pearl. Make me your illumined cave
of wonders. Make me your clever girl.

YEAR OF

Restless at the kitchen table, year of our Lord twenty twenty-four, year my words marched backward into my mouth and forward only when forgotten, year of the Stanley tumbler, year of the subtle but far-reaching machinations of neo-Marxism depending on who you ask, year of our lady of fuck around and find out, year of pundits, year of Doja Cat, year of royal family tabloid drama, year of literal and figurative warfare, bloodlust year, year of desire, year of frustrated desire, year of gradually excruciating guided identification of desires, year of my father unable to discuss that which is not the village council, year of the child, the laughing year of the wailing child, the domestic year, the exotic year, the year of everything turning to poetry, the year of poetry turning to nothing, the year of your turning to everything, the year of totality, the lost and found year, the year of the late bloom of the heart's silent madness, year of attending to various screens, year of continual scrolling, the unchurched year, the year of tallying ecclesial Latin absorbed by the body, the *pleni sunt coeli et terra gloria tua* year, the irreverent year, the year of tabula rasa and later perceptions of time, the year of the timely year, the seasonal year, the calendar year, year of annual infinity, the year of the erotic diminuendo, the yearless pleasured year of self, the wanton year, the may be out after hours year, the year of slow staircase ascents, the year of our Lord not yet come again, the year lavished on a boy, the year wasted on a man, the unmanned barely manageable one-woman year of kitchen table restlessness, the year of being trapped in a Word document, the year of being trapped in a word.

BOOK OF UNCOMMON PRAYER

Tome with a spine of real bone—the kind of thing
a dog might bury and dig up
and bury again.

Rufus wags his tail, avails himself of a warm
afternoon; trots in, proudly drops *Lord, it's all
feeling pretty fucked* on your spotless Persian.

He knows this is the book you need.

MASTER, MASTER

I was not a reluctant disciple. I knelt
quickly, touched my brow to your sandal
quickly, waited for you to raise gently

my chin with thumb and forefinger, to hold
my gaze, hold sway. I want to do everything
your way. I know you know

I'm a teachable creature, malleable,
with space enough on my tongue for a long
pilgrimage, for many heavy tomes.

Master, master, my love of you has been
the death of artifice, you emptied my sleeves
of their tricks and filled my heart

with your own image. I will spread
my cloak beneath your feet, eat
from your tree of knowledge, lovely

to my sight. It is fruitful for me so to do,
meet and right—only pardon my eagerness,
my vast appetite.

BLIZZARD

Wide white world,
worthy or unworthy—
I love you.

Snow that so covers
rutted roadsides, my
brown gullies and gulfs,
is it

Christlike?
Is that too quaint?

Corrosive Christ, eat
through these sins, or don't you
love me?

Flakes fall, stakes rise
in proportion to mistakes—

can I look like this seamless
world I see? Every

sound makes me jump, I think
it's trumpets, I think here come

the horsemen. I want snow Jesus,
not acid Jesus. I emerge

dirty in the godmelt, is there
a gospel for that?

GOOD ANIMAL

I was your good animal,
your tiger eye. You were my

one ruling
roar. I was your

jungle smut but far
more, a like-minded
beast.

Come palm come fern come vine
we said, *come green*

to greater green, come enflesh

our feast. So fast! I was your
good animal, not best. Not

first, not last.

HEART TALKS

Last night I tried to pray
heal my loneliness
which is not repentance, exactly.

I feel it most when my heart talks
to itself. This happens
more often than I'd like, like yesterday
as the geese flew their evening arc
over the cow-pond. *Who are you,*

it said; *who will you become?* Then,

your soul has a thousand mirrors,
and you are standing in all of them,
what a waste, what a shame. So
I tried again—

heal my loneliness
heal my loneliness
heal my loneliness

as I spoke many pairs of wings
moved together, spread,
broke briefly the horizon's
solitary line—broke mine.

TWO TAKES

1. *Hades Takes a Goodie*

Hades, Persephonize my suffering.
From its eternal winter, make the Spring
to succor whirling earth and those above,
and give me the dark scorching of your love—
let Beauty crush me as the serpent's head
and I will sing new songs among the dead.

2. *Hades Takes a Baddie*

Hades hurt me good, let finer pitchfork points
be understood in skin. Take me to a dive bar,
and I'll sing karaoke hymns in the dry
martini hour of our mirth. Give me a death
better than birth. How dirty do you like it?
Eat these olives on my tongue, oh Hades let's
have fun—I'm only going down if you go down.
Let my eyes lose sight of mama's harvest; give me
the collar. Give me the crown.

KNOWN

And Adam knew his wife, who through the knowing
bore Cain. You're handsy in the Uber,
having known me all afternoon though
what I will bear as a result is not
yet clear—you tied your hair
to the purpose, preparatory, eager
as the gull's beak golden-wide, meal-open.
The city glitters and ticks and we share
breath, break bread, lie down with
time up our sleeves, antediluvian at best—
the flood looms.

Should I now conceive and bear sorrow
when the seed was sown in joy; joy
for our interlocking fingers, my lingering
longing in the lore-soaked sheets—
no one to tell how your eyes were so soft,
knew me so well?

INNOCENCE

was a tiny bird in my open palm,
        and twice as frail. It flutters

still in memory—how I crimsoned
        when my older cousins first

began to curse, new speech rupturing the driven
        snow of my ear-drums; if I was shown a ripe

and splitting plum my mind would conjure scenes
        of sandwiches and chips or beans.

Now the frail bird of that innocence—
        a feathered ghost that sings—beats

its spectral wings against my closed window. Inside,
        between profanities, I hum with lidded eyes

like the plucked string of a lute. Pure fruit.

DRIFTING

The message bobbing, battered
in a bottle on the sea of God, my cries
sunk in the salt of the divine. Brine
to brine I greet you Lord, assaulted
by your vastness, tendered
on your tender waves that toss
my glass to shore. O that you
would read me! Again I wade
into the deep of you, cast anew
my hidden heart. Unchart
to unmap, it floats. This light plays
on holy water and my sight.

Am I asking the wrong sea—
are you the message drifting
through the dark ocean of me?

WHAT WAS THE BEST YOU EVER HAD?

I still have the shape of it—
him in the room like a wolf,
my shell-pink swell beneath
his lupine tongue, our too-late
awareness of lost hours;
the day also eaten.

WHAT IS MEMORY, IF NOT TESTAMENT?

Distracted with some menial task or else
my nose in a book or too much
in the mirror—I wasn't watching.
I didn't see your tenderness exactly
go, didn't notice if it tried to catch my eye
before the last. It's possible
tenderness left reluctantly, looked back
in case. Or maybe it just hurried out—I'm not
sure, but no spring could emerge in the winter
we became. A while now since your fine mouth
formed my name. Is memory the realm
of the real? Everyone says no. But I remember
you, tender as a new
testament, especially
late at night, and in the morning.
I recall it as a kind of good childhood—golden
and remote. If not quite real, true.

MY FAVORITE MEN

The men in my life
have a lot to say.
burn everything he ever gave you
Ok—

I like a man as a mother,
a drain to spiral down;
I like a man as an ace
that won't fit neatly up my sleeve,
I like a man as Jesus—behold
the man
saying *get off Instagram*, *leave
and cleave*, saying *you can't lose
your salvation*, saying *god damn,
baby*, saying *kiki do you love me*,

saying *goodbye*, and sometimes
not bothering. Men like it
when you follow directions,

unless the directions come
from another man; men like
to be held in your esteem
and in other high holy places
and in low ones.

My favorite men are dead,
mostly; saying
*stop this day and night with me
and you shall possess the origin of all poems*

In flight, Drake in the aisle and Whitman
near the window, obviously—me
smack in the middle. Or even better,
catch me drawing water

from a coke machine—Christ saying
go, call your husband, and come back—
shoving ten bucks in the station
attendant's hand, returning. My Shepherd
shutting his lordly eyes.

BETWEEN THE JAWS

Say you want to lick each
brain you like—what then? Say
some men enjoy your lips
brushing their thoughts, say some
have tongues like wonderful ideas
but you're only slightly into that—

you don't care to seek the mouth
or bed until you've had the head.
Say some men bare minds like teeth, say

you want to go out in a blaze
of synapses between the jaws of genius,
queen of the pyre—is this disordered
desire? Would you fare better
feeling up biceps? Tracing hairlines?
Cradling an *Encyclopædia Britannica*
between your thighs?

SALOME

The man desires the girl—

half my kingdom, half my kingdom

(whole my folly, O Eros, O god
of oblivion)

the girl defers to the mother, the mother
demands blood—

He fawns.

Whatever you ask now I will give,
my dancer, my dancer…

Would there were a way
to make her say

wings! The king's to shelter me,
and failing that, my own to fly

this inhospitable gospel. In my dreams
it is not too late: a smiling servant brings

a head of lettuce on a golden plate.

SWAMP CREED

To the One who from the Father
and the Son proceeds, who is worshipped
and glorified, speaking through mouths
of prophets and reeds on which
small marsh birds rest—

it seems to me that Need,
not Death, is the great
destroyer of worlds, now I am
become.

You are already in your kingdom—
I seek no remembrance.

Reach down and fill
my mouth; fill all until
my name is new, is
Needlessness.

The mouths of reeds look empty,
yet you—forever holy, forever passing
through—wet them, linger
inside them.

MOSES

I was very briefly a rhyme, you were
the reason. I've reverted in time
to riddle—something unanswerable,
a tree yielding out of season, a bush
burning white in the wilderness,
unconsumed, undevoured.

And you came again
to the threshold of this land promised
to you, flowing with milk and honey,
but you would not enter.

And the silk of my days was torn,
and nothing rhymed, and still
you were the reason.

LEAF BLOWER

So somber, amber the dying
summer's ember. I clutch
November. If you could see how red
this red. Flood comes color,
knocking everything alive before
deadening smooth and brown
as dusk. I dream down in a russet
wood, wake in one too. People
are out walking here, walking
beneath heavenly hosts of leaves—
amen I say to you, salvation
will catch us up in its great rake,
we will be bagged by glory, bound
and gagged by glory, which shuts
the mouth and stills the hands.
You with eyes to see how red
and fair this red—go, and let
my people stare. No hush now,
too flushed with gales, this air—
O God, God's rosehip lips, their
movement…

TO THE OTHER HALEY IN THE CAB

Madness can be elegant—
there's Sylvia Plath, there's
Mrs. Doubtfire, there's Lear.

Mostly you're not sure what
you're doing here, with all this sanity
banal as a teacup, your grief
corresponding to reason.

You can have woes, you can have
whoa whoa whoas, you can have both.
You can share a cab with someone
that shares your name, spelling
and everything. You can find

a boy and lose a boy, birth
a boy, raise a boy, wed yourself
to a boy—it can be all boys
all the time. Not even this
is enough to *hiss hiss hiss*
you into madness, to go *'ban, 'ban,
Caliban* monstering mad. You can

taste lucidity, sense sense like plaque
between the bared mind's figurative
teeth, you can bequeath a poem
to the other Haley in the cab—

so cute, so friendly, so ready to chat
while you slunk, rat-like and distracted
by the unbroken camel's back furious
to see you could take yet
more, endure it cleanly.

You can hate your strength,
you can know for certain no one
will find you with your head
in the oven, that no one will write
"the rest is posthumous." You can even
re-read *Ariel* while playing Ariel—remain
sane as a stone, as algebra, as a diplomat.

BACK YARD

Green and deathless kingdom, can you be
a foretaste? My tongue bears
only so much, can imagine only
so much bliss. Still, the thrill
of each light-locked leaf, the many-
birded trill transmits the almost
tangible promise.

ROOFTOP

You say the seminary students
come up here to smoke weed,
which makes sense. And I'm here
by myself now, with you. If
you're lonely enough, the city

is a wilderness. The body too.
I'm aware it's windy tonight
and within me, it's cold—knowing
I want to be held, but can't ask. Every
grain of sand has lowered itself down
our hourglass. As far as asking for things,
time's up. There must be a bell and a clock
in this tower. Let it ring:

I'll pass through the buzzing streets
like John the Baptist, eating locusts
and wild honey alone alone alone
preparing a new lord's way
without a care and held—finally
held—by my garment of camel's hair.

LAMB LEGS

In late April my boy
runs on wide green

come back with natural laws
from brown ground. There are
whole days of this,

days gone with his flying
lamb legs that pause, offering
a dandelion and *mama why
do bad guys exist?*

I'm drawing nearer to the middle
of my life. I have this boy
and dandelions to show for it,
which—God—is it enough?

No, says one voice, even as
another says *it's immeasurable.*

SUBSERVIENT

I am drawn from your rib.

God plucked me
from your chest,
could thrust me in again.
Since we are dust, love,
tell me what sort of dust
to be. Shall I settle on you, or
shall you breathe me in and later
cough me up, wiping me from
your wet lips, from the brow
that sweats for its bread?

LESSON

Ok: are you available to be the ripe
fig of my days by chance? Maybe
take your tongue to the bruised floor
of my being and tell me what you taste?
All my chaste years rattle around
down there, asking what they were for.
I say let's live up to any hype
that's left. Do you love my cleft
stick? If you know how—
teach me.

INTO GOLD

—at your feet I have laid
this pretty way of speaking

grace to you:
swans' necks, violins,
many pillars of white marble,
the softening of harsh words,
a hovering hummingbird and his jewel tone,
snow

—it is the best and only alchemy I know

peace to you:
hushed fields, rain in the shipyard, evensong,
a lover's breath released, silver harness bells,
stone

—for the transformation of matter
language alone

MAYBE WELCOME IT,

the way sorrow sweeps, seeps, sows,
reaps, eats what it grows, the way
sorrow knows, savors, flows, flavors
all it touches, the way it clutches
firm as any lover come to hover
over what has been, the way sorrow
gets in, paws, draws quick
as any flame, remains the same, re-wilds
tame things, flings, takes, breaks,
shakes, flakes into itself without
dissolving, the way sorrow involving
some heart with yours floors, pours
emptiness from fullness—

just maybe. Just try.

INKED

You, from the beginning,
relishing occlusives. Making
and re-making your skin
from language; feeling each
curving vowel, every plosive.

Breath here, gone, deferred, come.
A series of advents, deaths, ascensions.
This is the wind you want—

warm—hovering over naked
syllables. And you want permission
to want. You get all worked up
for authority, a primary text.

Your heart has chased the hart
of exposure through wooded veins,
traced your own etymology: the words

that formed the words that form
the word you are—the word
a reader's tongue might enwrap
and taste and see,

flesh dissolving into sexed
vocabulary, a thousand silver
letters, your inked and glowing
intercourse with life.

UTTERANCES

I bring you, Lord, ten-thousand
shabby utterances, brittle and rough
as any bottle-brush. Would they had
been beautiful!

I sucked your glowing coal—
thought of your burning
in my burning, thought

my finger-puppet tongue
might reach the ancient, flaming
pillar of your speech.
I sucked, I burned, I thought.

But articulation—all—labors
and lives beneath the Fall.

DADDY DELILAH

Simple—so—to overthrow the spent
and sleeping man, to run his hair
through this little loom.

I am a sweet, a soft, demurring
doom, my pillowed thighs your
pillar-practice your demise
your sapped and sapping
strength. My love my love oh
look me in the eyes—

who's your daddy now?

LAST RITES

Once, you told me that words are spells,
that conversation is a sacrament.

Back then we could really *communicate*—
ever seen a flower unfurl? It all used to feel
so good, so heard, so sunward.

But the ex-communicated
do not receive the sacraments.
Bet gutsy ones still ask.

And when I finally say
all I want to, which way do your great
cathedral doors swing?

Forgive me father for I have
gone on speaking.

THE TELLING

In the loud presence of honeysuckle,
crow-cawed and coo-doved, cloud-
swallowed now beneath the swallow's
wing—I'm sure: creation is God's speech.
And the particular
vim of the leaping doe's
a verb. As all going must,
it tells of Him.

ALMS

Christ tucked between the floorboards of the burning
    barn, pale
frail wafer Christ, Christ of tapered longings and split
ends—swift ends cut like wood like corners
like hair—hoarfrost Christ, September Christ of crab
apples and chrysanthemums, Christ of minds bent
double retching and reeling, of hearts curled up
like an old dog's tail, scarlet Christ, Christ of mended
shoes, Christ of the chalice and grail, billowing
sail Christ, Christ of the stomped lantern fly:

I think I
came to beg for something—

ACKNOWLEDGMENTS

With special thanks and deep gratitude to *Cassandra Voices*, *Ekstasis*, *Luna Luna*, *Pink Disco Magazine*, *Reformed Journal*, *Solum Journal*, and *t'ART*, in which several of these poems first appeared.

ABOUT THE AUTHOR

Haley Hodges received her MFA in Creative Writing from Seattle Pacific University. She holds additional qualifications in music and theology from Hope College, Shenandoah Conservatory, and Oxford University. Native to West Michigan, she lives in West Virginia with her husband and son.

ABOUT ORISON BOOKS

Orison Books is a 501(c)3 non-profit literary press focused on the life of the spirit from a broad and inclusive range of perspectives. We seek to publish books of exceptional poetry, fiction, and non-fiction from perspectives spanning the spectrum of spiritual and religious thought, ethnicity, gender identity, and sexual orientation.

As a non-profit literary press, Orison Books depends on the support of donors. To find out more about our mission and our books, or to make a donation, please visit www.orisonbooks.com.

Orison Books is deeply grateful to our recurring annual donors for sustaining our important work. If you'd like to make a recurring or one-time contribution, please visit
www.orisonbooks.com/support-us.

Sustainers' Circle

Carol Dines
Keith Flynn
Laura & Barry Rand
Lee Stockdale
Anonymous

Advocates' Circle

David Ebenbach
Bruce Spang
Anonymous

Supporters' Circle

Nickole Brown
Richard Chess
Beth Juliar

Friends' Circle

Paige Gilchrist
Alida Woods
Anonymous

www.ingramcontent.com/pod-product-compliance
Lightning Source LLC
Chambersburg PA
CBHW020443090526
44586CB00045B/834